The Mystery of Matt Talbot

Father Morgan Costelloe
Vice-Postulator of the
Cause of the Ven. Matt Talbot

MESSENGER PUBLICATIONS
37, Lower Leeson Street,
Dublin 2.

Telephone: 01 676 7491
Fax: 01 661 1606
E-Mail: sales@messenger.ie

Nihil Obstat: Hilary Lawton, S.J.
                   Censor Theol. Deput.
Imprimi Potest: Dermitius,
                   Archiep. Dublinen. Hib. Primas.
Dublini, Die: 18 Dec 1981

ISBN 1-872245-57-9

10-6-88

10-7-91

1-5-00

20-9-03

Printed in the Republic of Ireland
© Messenger Publications
37 Lower Leeson Street, Dublin 2.

The cover photograph was taken in T & C Martin's about 1918.
Matt Talbot is on the extreme left. It is reproduced with the kind
permission of the Archdiocese of Dublin.

The Mystery of Matt Talbot

Introduction

Many years ago I spoke to an old lady about Matt Talbot. She lived in a tenement, long since demolished, directly behind Dublin's Gresham Hotel. Matt Talbot had lived nearby. 'If I done the things that he done,' she said in a broad Dublin accent, 'they would put me in the madhouse.

As the Vice-Postulator of the Cause of Venerable Matt Talbot, I have heard similar remarks in Ireland and abroad. There is an aspect of his spirituality that appears forbidding and mysterious. Where did he get the idea for his fasts, his long night vigils and his awesome asceticism? The answer is that, under the guidance of a spiritual director, he imitated the life of the monks in the early Irish monasteries.

This booklet is not another biography of Matt Talbot. It presupposes that the reader has heard his life story which is well told in Mary Purcell's *Remembering Matt Talbot* or her pamphlet *The Making of Matt Talbot*. The purpose of this booklet is to explain the spiritual programme that led him to close union with God.

Many Irish persons today have lost a sense of history. They can name some of the great monasteries like Clonard, Glendalough and Clonmacnois, which became world-famous through the visit of Pope John Paul II in 1979, but they know little about the life of the monks who lived there. They go on pilgrimage to Lough Derg, known as St Patrick's Purgatory, without realising that this penitential exercise has its roots in early Irish spirituality which has always emphasised the need for penance: 'Unless you repent you will all likewise perish' *(Lk 13:3)*.

The Irish monks who lived out this belief, were for the most part lay-brothers rather than priests. Their treasures, like the *Book of Kells* and the *Ardagh Chalice*, are part of our heritage. Their devotion to prayer, to Sacred Scripture, to Mary, the Mother of God, and to missionary effort is all part of our spiritual tradition, as Sir William Butler reminds us: 'Let us remember that these old teachers belong entirely to us. It was not a strange race of beings who thus toiled and taught and triumphed. They were our own glorious people. The dust of many of them is in our midst and the simple words in which they asked our prayers can still be read upon their mouldering tombstones' *(Ireland: Its Saints and Scholars, J. M. Flood: Introduction)*.

Irish Monasticism

One of the extraordinary events in our history was the widespread interest in the monastic life which manifested itself within a hundred years of the death of St Patrick. By the end of the sixth century there were thirty major monastic settlements scattered through the country and we are told of young men and women flocking to consecrate their lives to God.

At first a hermit would set up his cell in a secluded spot to communicate with God in private; but the news would spread and others would gather around him to seek his advice on prayer. Eventually small self-sufficient communities were formed and the hermit's life, in the strict sense, was almost a thing of the past. The spiritual acorn became a mighty oak, some monasteries having as many as four thousand people, including overseas students.

Glendalough and Clonmacnois became university cities of their day, while remaining like all the monasteries, places of prayer, solitude and study. As they grew, extra buildings were added near the original monks' cells, the church, the refectory, the kitchen, a room for washing, a guest house: a school with a lecture hall and a scriptorium where scribes practised their art. It would do justice to a modern development plan.

Life in the monasteries was summed up by St Columbanus as: 'pray daily, fast daily, study daily, work daily' (*Opera,* p. 24). The great monks, who were proposed as models, were those who persevered in strict obedience to their Abbot, over forty or fifty years.

This characteristic was expressed with earthy wisdom by MacUige of Lismore who said that a monk might be condemned for his excessive humility or for his fasting but he could never be criticised for being 'too persevering'. 'Perseverance in holiness', said St Fursa, 'is the anvil of piety.' This incessant search for holiness demanded the discipline of the body as well as of the mind.

The Irish monks believed strongly in bringing the body firmly into subjection to reason and to the service of God. They held that if they could reduce its need for food, sleep and comfort to a minimum they would produce maximum response to God's inspiration for prayer and charity.

Means Towards An End

Asceticism was the order of the day in monastic Ireland. It was so strict that scholars look to the Eastern Church to find anything like it. Innumerable prostrations and genuflections during prayer were common. The cross-vigil, which required the monk to kneel without support with his arms stretched out in the form of a cross, was the recommended posture. Fasts on bread and water lasted for days on end. In case a monk should be deluded by pride to undertake too many acts of mortification, he was cautioned to choose a spiritual director. This spiritual father was given the beautiful Irish title of 'anam-chara', which translated into English, means 'soul-friend'. He was both confessor and advisor, who constantly reminded the monk that austerity was not an end in itself, only a means towards closer union with God. The need for an individual spiritual director was considered so important that novices were told that a monk without one was 'like a body without a head'.

Well-Tried Faith

Brehon laws governed the life of Irish men and women outside the monasteries during the fifth and sixth centuries. Violations of civil law were severely punished. The monks realised this and it seemed logical that violation of God's law should incur grave punishment also.

Penance for sins was harsh. Capital crimes, like perjury and murder, were punished by exile for life. Lesser violations of the law were punished by fasting on bread and water for any period from two days to several years. Sins were confessed privately to a priest in the Sacrament of Penance; but imperfections and violations of the monastic Rule were confessed publicly to the Abbot and the community. The Abbot imposed a penance for failure to observe the Rule, and, depending on the gravity of the offence, this could range from confinement to one's cell, to extra prayers or corporal punishment.

Such a strict life shocked the Benedictine monks when they eventually met their Irish counterparts on the Continent. It provoked a comment from the modern scholar, Daniel Rops, reminiscent of the remark which the lady made about Matt Talbot: 'There was nothing easy about life in these (Irish monastic) communities. Their ways of ascetic piety would be regarded by most men of the twentieth century as quite insane'. He goes on: 'All the monks submitted to a penitential regime, which seems astounding to our easy-going ways. The ideal of penance was what these men set out to find in cells lost in the midst of woods or in the most desolate countryside. The finest examples of a well-tried faith were forged here' (*Introduction to Ireland: Isle of Saints*, by C & B Cerebeland-Salagnance).

The 'Hard' Man

The idea of Irish monasticism was far from Matt Talbot's mind when he took a pledge to abstain from drink for three months. It was a Saturday afternoon in 1884. He was broke and his friends refused to buy him a drink. Barney, as he was known to his drinking pals in O'Meara's public house, was certainly not a religious man. He went to Mass every Sunday, often through the haze of a hang-over, but he had not been to Confession, nor to Holy Communion, for some years. In build, he was small, five feet six inches tall, tough and stocky.

He was a 'hard' man, in the Dubliner's sense of the word - a hard worker and a hard drinker. He knew no half-measure. All activities were undertaken with whole-hearted commitment. He lived for alcohol. He went to Confession that fateful Saturday afternoon to a priest in Holy Cross College, Clonliffe, and promised to abstain from alcoholic drink for three months. His determination to keep that pledge may have sprung initially from hurt pride, but it immediately presented serious problems such as Matt had not foreseen. He had to overcome the terrifying withdrawal symptoms of alcoholism, which, in those days, were not fully understood by the medical profession. Moreover, until that time he had spent all his spare time in O'Meara's public house.

What would he do now after work? This is a problem which all alcoholics have to face during the early stages of their recovery. Although his achievements at school were poor enough, Matt was an intelligent man. So he went for a walk to pass the time. But where would he rest when he got tired? To turn into a public house would be disastrous. He sat at the back of a church. Battling with nausea, hallucinations and with the depression which obsessed him, he begged God to help him. Despite his poor effort at formal prayer, Matt Talbot found serenity and security during these vital three months, before the Blessed Sacrament in St Joseph's Church, Berkeley Road and in St Francis Xavier's Church, Gardiner Street. It was an unlikely beginning of a deep intimacy between him and his Saviour that would bridge the next forty years.

To strengthen his resolution further, he decided to attend Mass and receive Holy Communion every day before work. It was a revolutionary idea! In Ireland of the 1880's a good-living layman went to the altar just twice a year, at Easter and at Christmas. A nun or a Brother with religious vows went only on Sundays. Matt arrived at 5 a.m. Mass in Gardiner Street church every morning and received Holy Communion. There were occasions during these crucial months when his resolution reached breaking-point. He later described that time as a 'hell on earth', but thanks to the grace of God and his innate stubbornness he remained sober. The first hurdle on his road to recovery had been cleared. He renewed the pledge for six months and then took it for life.

Change of Life Style

From 1884 onwards Matt Talbot adopted a new life style. He had steady employment on the docks. His willingness to work hard for long hours assured him of work when it was available. To fill in his time after hours and to satisfy his increasing interest in religious matters, he joined the Third Order of St Francis attached to the Franciscan Church, Merchant's Quay.

He continued to go to Mass and Holy Communion every morning in the Jesuit church, Gardiner Street, near his home and became a member of its Workingmen's Sodality dedicated to Our Lady Immaculate. Its director was Father James Walsh, S.J. Matt went to confession to him or to Father Tom Murphy, S.J., a well-known preacher, every week. In the days before radio and television, many poor people attended Sodalities and Confraternities. Such meetings were religious and social occasions, the sermons providing topics of conversation the following day. His father and brothers were drinking heavily and there were rowdy scenes and strong language. Eventually, Matt left home and went to live alone in a tenement flat at the top of 18 Upper Rutland Street.

At one stage, he considered getting married. A girl proposed to him and he told her that he would make a Novena and give his decision. She got a firm refusal. Matt returned with the extraordinary explanation that Our Lady had told him not to get married. It is not certain that Father Walsh was more than Matt's regular confessor. There is evidence that he helped him greatly to remain sober and encouraged him to overcome illiteracy. Although illiterate when he left school, he gradually learned to read and write. Matt became friendly with another priest, Dr. Michael Hickey, later Monsignor, of Holy Cross College, Clonliffe, who played a major role in his spiritual formation. An enlightened confessor and scholar, he became Matt's director, a true 'anam-chara' guiding him in the way of Irish spirituality.

Hymns From The Top Flat

This life-long friendship gave rise to some unusual situations. During his talks to the seminarians in the College, Dr Hickey would confide occasionally that he knew 'the holiest man in Dublin whose prayers are always answered'. The most perceptive among them wondered if this was the small bowed-shouldered man who made his way up the winding roadway through the College grounds every Saturday and was ushered, not into the parlours where all penitents went, but up the stairs to Dr Hickey's room. Matt enjoyed a unique privilege. The seminarians' surprise was equalled by that of the people of Rutland Street at the frequent sight of a ruddy-faced priest climbing the broken stairway at No. 18 to visit Mr Talbot. The two friends would sometimes sing hymns together, mingling their praise of God with cries of the baby in the front drawing-room and the shouts of the drunken man in the back-parlour. Had the neighbours realised that the room at the top of the house was in fact a replica of a 'monastic cell', they could not have been more astonished. For its occupant was seeking the closest union with God through the means adopted by Irish monks a thousand years before.

When we consider the principal elements in the life of the early Irish monk, it is easy to see how they were paralleled in the life of this Dublin workman. These were: *prayer, fasts, mortifications, work, study, devotion to Our Lady and missionary drive*. Let us consider each in turn.

THE IRISH WAY

Praising God

Prayer in its various forms - vocal, mental and contemplative - is the way to closer union with God. The Sacrifice of the Mass is the supreme act of worship in the Catholic Church and Sunday Mass was the climax of a week of prayer in every Irish monastery. In the sixth century, Mass was celebrated only on Sundays and on solemn feast-days. There was a special Mass at Easter and at Christmas and on the anniversaries of Ss. Peter and Paul, St. Martin and of the founder of each monastery. Permission for a Mass was given also on hearing of the death of a friend of the monastery. But the six weekdays were generally considered as a prolonged preparation for the Sunday celebration. Adamnan, the biographer of St Colmcille, reveals the tremendous devotion of the Irish monks to the Mass; we learn that, while they stood right through the Eucharistic liturgy, they prostrated themselves in silence and reverence during the consecration. Although there was no compulsion, the monks were strongly counselled to receive Holy Communion whenever they attended Mass.

The monks at St Columbanus's monastery at Luxeuil in France were told to make three prostrations on their way to the altar. Frequent confession to one's director, even once a day, was also recommended by St Columbanus in a graphic phrase: 'As a floor is swept once a day with a broom, so the soul should be cleansed once a day by confession'. The great daily prayer was the public recitation of the Divine Office. The monks came together seven times a day, including the early hours of the morning, to praise God, chanting the Psalms and reading passages from Sacred Scripture. There was no uniformity in the recitation of the Divine Office in the sixth century, but there was no lack of generosity in prayer. St Columbanus, for instance, prescribed twenty-four psalms for the night Office during the short summer nights and thirty-six for the long winter ones.

The long penitential psalms, like Psalm 118, were very popular, interspersed with many genuflections and prostrations. The early Irish monks spent many hours each day praying in public. Spiritual reading was provided from the Gospels and spiritual books and St Columbanus recommended that after public prayer the monk should retire to his cell to meditate and to pray privately.

One Full Meal

Apart from the routine of prayer, the life of the Irish monk was one of continual self-denial. Each year three periods of forty days were observed as times of 'black fast'. These were: the customary period of Lent, another in preparation for Christmas - a prolonged Advent - and a period after Pentecost. A six week period after Easter was observed as one of great joy, and strict fasting was suspended. But with the exception of Eastertide, every Wednesday and Friday was a day of fast. The name given to these days in the Irish language tells its own story. Wednesday is *Dia Céadaoin*, which means the day of the first fast and Friday, *Dia hAoine*, the fasting day. During the fasts of forty days the monks were allowed only one meal a day consisting of bread, vegetables and water or milk. This meal was taken in the evening. But even at the best of times when two collations and one full meal were permitted, the menu was meagre: vegetables, such as beans and cabbage, flour mixed with water, fish or an egg, small fragments of bread that resembled hard biscuits, white sauce or milk

This kind of diet may dismay us of the 'three-meals-a-day' culture but as late as the 17th century many people of Ireland had only one meal a day. A letter to King Philip II from a Captain Cuellar, who arrived in Donegal with the Spanish Armada in 1589, describes Irishmen as being strong and agile, 'who ate but one meal a day and that at night; and their ordinary food is water, bread and butter. They drink sour milk, as they have no other beverage but water'. (*Letter of Captain Cuellar*, H. Sedgwick p. 69). Despite their meagre diet, the Irish monks were tough, fit men who sailed their leather boats to France and then tramped across the Continent as far as Italy and Bavaria.

Monks At Work

But prayer alone did not feed the monks. 'The monk is fed and clothed by the labour of his hands', a directive ran; and daily work was an obligation for all the monks from the Abbot to the most junior novice. All work was carried out in strict silence to maintain a spirit of recollection. Necessary communication was made by signs and there was a great variety of work. Some of the monks worked within the enclosure, e.g. the guestmaster, the miller and the baker. Craftsmen made the chalices, the patens and the Mass vestments.

Some of their workmanship is a source of wonder to us even today. They were joined by the scribes, those monks who copied the Bible and manuscripts. St Columcille is reputed to have made three hundred copies of the New Testament in his own hand. However, most of the monks worked in the fields, reclaiming land, digging ditches, fencing and draining. Some of them tended to the cows, very important animals, not just for their milk, but for their hides which were converted into boats, harness, ropes and shoes. Other monks worked in the garden to cultivate vegetables - cabbage, celery, parsnips, peas and beans. Much of the produce went to the poor and the guests of the monastery. Finally, if the monastery was situated - as many were - on an island or near a river, a group of monks would set out with their nets and their lines to catch fish. No meat was eaten.

And So To School

'Study daily' was St Columbanus's fourth recommendation. St Finnian of Clonard had a profound influence on the curriculum of monastic studies. He blended together the old Celtic scholarship, which pre-dated the arrival of St Patrick, and the Latin Christian studies, which came with our national apostle. The monastery became a type of early boarding school which attracted pupils from Ireland and abroad, some of whom became monks, while others returned home after a number of years and married. The curriculum included study of the Old and New Testament, geometry, rhetoric, grammar, arithmetic and Greek.

The teaching of the pupils by the teaching monks and the spiritual formation of novices were also classified as work. Generally speaking, the studies of the student monks centred on the Latin language, on theology in the widest sense, and on Sacred Scripture. This last was considered the most important; and as soon as a pupil had learned the Latin alphabet, vocabulary and grammar, he was given a psalter and required to learn part of it, at least, by heart. Since monks recited long Offices at night it helped to have memorised the Psalms, when artificial light was poor or non-existent. After the Psalms came portions of the Sacred Text, like St Matthew's Gospel and the Acts of the Apostles. For the more successful students there was an advanced course in all subjects. It was, therefore, little wonder that Ireland was given the title of 'The Island of Saints and Scholars'.

'Green' Martyrdom

At the end of a day of prayer, work and study the monk retired to his cell for sleep. He was allowed four hours rest on a pallet of straw and a pillow. We learn, however, that St Columcille and St Columbanus lay on a slab of stone and had a stone pillow. St Feichin of Fobar settled for a plank of wood and a wooden pillow.

This continual search for conquest of natural inclinations sprang from the conviction that a true follower of Jesus should renounce himself and lose his life for the sake of his Master. 'If any man would come after me, let him deny himself and take up his cross and follow me. For whoever would save his life will lose it; and whoever loses his life for my sake and the Gospel's will save it' *(Mark 8:34-35)*. The monk was a 'miles Christi', a soldier of Christ, who set out to conquer self in order to draw closer to God.

It was a kind of martyrdom, as the monks acknowledged. Few Irish monks suffered red martyrdom - shedding their blood for the sake of the Gospel - although St Killian and his companions did when they travelled to Wurtzburg in Germany. But all the Irish monks were expected to achieve what was called 'white' martyrdom - the renunciation of everything one loved, living in complete poverty of spirit

There was a higher stage on the way to perfection, however, for monks who performed additional penance by fasting and labour and sought the profoundest humility. The monks described this as 'green' martyrdom.

In recent times an Irish preacher commented that a religious novice ought to be as 'pliable as porridge and as humble as a doormat'. The old Irish monks would have understood that Professor Gabriel Le Bras answers those who find this emphasis on mortifications daunting: 'They must be studied, if they are to be properly understood, according to the mentality of the period', he writes. 'We must not stop at the 'letter' but make for the 'spirit' and recognise how the penitentials are witnesses and regulators of the structures and customs of Ireland; they held in the evolution of penance a role with a universal range; they responded to a practical conception of relations with God' (*The Irish Penitentials*, article in *The Miracle of Ireland*, by Daniel-Rops).

Pilgrims for Christ

The highest form of this 'green' martyrdom was voluntary exile for Christ. Having consulted their spiritual director, monks decided that they were called to this supreme act of sacrifice, and left their families and native land 'in search of salvation and solitude'. They were 'peregrini pro Christo' - pilgrims for Christ - who endured a kind of death before death, by freely leaving their loved ones forever to seek spiritual perfection for themselves and to bring the Gospel message to the pagans. They understood well the wrench that was involved.

'It is the parting of soul and body for a man to leave his kindred and his country and to go to strange, distant lands in exile and perpetual pilgrimage', we read in the *Life of St Columcille, (Old Ireland*, edited by Robert McNally, S.J.).

With childlike trust in the providence of God, they sailed their small leather boats at the mercy of sea and storm, first to Scotland and England and later to continental Europe. Following the historic 'Brendan Voyage' in 1976 when Tim Severin sailed an identical boat from Ireland to Newfoundland, some scholars accept the claim that St Brendan may have discovered America. There is no doubt, however, about the Irish monks' travels to Europe. St Columbanus, like another St Paul, travelled twice across France, up the Rhine to Switzerland, across Lake Constance to Austria, and founded his last monastery at Bobbio in Northern Italy. St Fergal and his companions went to Bavaria, St Fiacre to Brittany, St Killian to Germany, St Cathal to Italy and St Gall to Switzerland, just to mention the more famous.

Although the desire to preach the Gospel was secondary, in time, to their desire for solitude, evangelisation invariably followed. They established themselves as men of deep personal religion, lovers of learning and original thinkers. They influenced the lives of their neighbours with the peculiar traits of Irish spirituality, a directness in prayer, spiritual direction and frequent confession. They brought a human touch: a love of children and of nature.

Although the 'pilgrimage for Christ' was highly regarded, it is a comment on their common sense that the Irish monks considered that it was neither desirable nor beneficial for everyone.

The Book of Lismore tells us that there were three kinds of pilgrimage. The first:leaving one's country for the love of God and forsaking vice for virtue; the second: leaving one's country without change of heart - a sheer waste of time; and the third: having the desire to go on pilgrimage when the call of duty demands that the monk stay at home.

Queen of Ireland

Besides devotion to the Mass and to the Divine Office, certain distinctive characteristics of Irish spirituality developed from the prayer-life of the early Irish monks. Fr Diarmuid O Laoghaire, S.J. enumerates a few in his essay, '*Old Ireland: Her Spirituality*'. They were: devotion to Christ, Our Lord, and to the Blessed Trinity; a tender love for the Son of Mary and a devotion to his Mother, Mary, to his Bride, the Church and to its liturgical life.

Their understanding of Our Lady's role in redemption was quite remarkable. They taught that her place in our salvation corresponded to Eve's role in our fall: she achieved by her obedience to God's will what our first parents lost through their disobedience. Mary was next to her Son in the realm of grace and the common reference to Jesus in the monastic prayer was under the title of 'Son of Mary'.

As students of the Irish language know, it bestows unique honour on Our Lady to this day. While other women bearing the name 'Mary' have it translated as Maire, the Blessed Virgin alone has a special form, *Muire*.

Today Ireland's national Marian shrine at Knock, Co Mayo - the goal of the Pope's visit in 1979 - is called *Cnoc Mhuire*. A poem of 150 verses to correspond to the Psalter was written in honour of Our Lady by an Irish monk, Blathmac, son of Cu Brettan, about 700 A. D. In it he invites Mary to share with him her grief - her 'keen' - at the death of her Son. Towards the end of this poem he makes a reference, to which we will return later:

For you, bright Mary, I shall go as guarantor:
anyone who shall say the full 'keen' shall have his reward.
I call you with true words, Mary, beautiful queen, that we may
hold converse together to console your heart's darling.

Mary's own prayer, the Magnificat *(Lk. 1:46-55)*, was a great favourite. The monks held that 'it is fitting that the words which came from the lips of the Virgin Mary, when she conceived by the Holy Spirit at the angel's greeting, should be the crown and conclusion of all those prayers which praise God and implore His pardon'.

THE MYSTERY OF MATT TALBOT

When we recall and ponder over the principal aspects of the spirituality of the Irish monks, we can understand better Matt Talbot's way to God. A great development had taken place over the centuries in the Church's appreciation of the Blessed Eucharist as a means towards holiness. It came to be realised that through this sacrament Jesus is present in his Church in a manner that surpasses all others. And since it contains Christ himself the Eucharist enables the individual to build up a close, personal relationship with his Saviour through the prayer of adoration, of thanksgiving, of reparation and of petition.

As century succeeded century more emphasis was placed on the desirability of daily Mass, daily reception of Holy Communion and visits to the Eucharistic Christ reserved in the tabernacle. The Second Vatican Council expressed the Church's faith and veneration for the mystery of the Eucharist. In 1965 Pope Paul VI wrote his encyclical *'Mysterium Fidei'* requesting priests to 'tirelessly promote the cult of the Eucharist, the focus where all other forms of piety must ultimately emerge'. He went on to explain that 'the Eucharist is reserved in the churches and oratories as in the spiritual centre of a religious community or of a parish, yes, of the universal Church'. Matt Talbot would have appreciated these comments as his new life of prayer, of penance, of study and of work centred around Christ in the Eucharist

'Old Reliable'

After the faltering beginning in St Joseph's church where he pleaded for the grace to remain sober, Matt built up a phenomenal devotion to Jesus in the Blessed Eucharist. When he was not working he was praying and when he was praying he was usually in an obscure corner of a church.

The friendship that he once found in O'Meara's pub was now replaced by an intimate companionship in the house of God. He continued to attend Mass and to receive Holy Communion at 5 o'clock Mass every morning in Gardiner Street Church. But when the time of this first Mass was changed to 6.15 Matt discovered that he was unable to return home for his breakfast and get to work in time, so he changed his job. Even during the Easter Rising of 1916 he made his way through military barricades to attend Mass. Sunday was D-Day. He went to first Mass and stayed in the church until the last Mass concluded with Benediction. Since he was obliged to fast from midnight in order to receive Holy communion, he did not have his breakfast until after 1.30 p.m.

Occasionally he moved from one church to another on Sundays, depending on where his various Sodalities met. He might slip away from the Jesuit Church, Gardiner Street to the Franciscan Church, Merchant's Quay or to the Dominican Church, Dominick Street.

He made himself as inconspicuous as possible, a small, poor man. He never used a prayer book but prayed with his eyes shut. He knelt erect in the bench, hour after hour, with his hands joined in front of him. He did not allow them to rest on the seat in front of him and so remained upright without support. He did not stand for the Gospel, a habit he learned from a saint to retain recollection. To the members of the Franciscan Church choir, who saw him from the gallery huddled in deep prayer, he was affectionately known as the 'old reliable'. His visits to a church were not limited to Mass time. He paid a visit to the Blessed Sacrament on his way to work, 'to see the Lord on the way down', as he said, and again after work 'to see the Lord on the way home'. Remembering that as a rule he returned to a church after his evening meal for a Sodality meeting, he saw a lot of the Lord.

Lost in Prayer

His little room at 18 Upper Rutland Street had the bare necessities of a monastic cell. He had an iron bedstead, a chair, a table, a crucifix and a few holy pictures. His bed covering was a sheet and a half blanket, supplemented by an old sack during the cold winter nights. When his Sodality meeting ended he returned to his room to pray before a large crucifix and to read spiritual books before retiring for the night.

Few persons saw him praying privately at home. His sister, Susan, was an exception. 'He sometimes had his arms crossed on his breast', she said. 'During his free time he was never off his knees'. Her mother, old Mrs. Talbot, spent her last twelve years with Matt in his flat. She kept a discreet silence about what she saw, but she once confided to her daughter that she saw Matt kneeling erect either on the bed, or on the floor, with his hands outstretched. She would ask him at first; 'Is anything the matter, Matt?', but he would not answer. She concluded that he was in ecstasy. Others who saw him praying before the Blessed Sacrament, got the same impression.

The Word of God

A study of the Bibles which Matt had in his room shows that he had a particular devotion to the long penitential psalms. There are heavy markings of the 50th psalm, the *Miserere*: 'Have mercy on me, O God, according to thy great mercy;' of the 101st Psalm: 'Hear, O Lord, my prayer; and let my cry come to thee', and of the 142nd Psalm. The Psalms, as a whole, appear to have been Matt's favourite prayers. But he had other prayers too: long litanies, which were freely available in leaflet or in booklet form. He wrote his favourite ejaculations on scraps of paper for example, 'How I long that Thou mayest be master of my heart, my Lord Jesus' or 'My God, my great God, my Life, my Love, my Glory'. 'Mary, Mother of Jesus, pray for me'.

The Good Queen

Thanks to his mother's secret observations, we get a glimpse of another of Matt's devotions, which was dear to the Irish monks - his fervent love of Mary, the Mother of God. She told her daughter, Susan, that she was convinced that he saw the Blessed Virgin. She overheard him regularly having intimate conversations with her, but she wished this fact to remain a family secret. Matt never referred to these conversations, but he had a habit of saying: 'No one knows the good Queen that she is to me'. It was a title that Blathmac, the monk, discovered over a thousand years before. Matt's moment of grace, outside O'Meara's public house, occurred on a Saturday - a day that the Church has traditionally dedicated to the Blessed Virgin - and he was sure that he could not have kept his pledge without her help.

Unaware of the reason for this, the priest who usually received Matt's contributions sent him Christmas greetings in 1924 and added that since he had not heard from him for some time, he hoped that he was not ill. Matt had some pennies saved, 'for a special occasion'. They amounted to thirty shillings (€1.90) and in the shaky hand of a sick man he wrote what has become a famous letter:

'Matt Talbot have done no work for past 18 months. I have been sick and given over by priest and doctor. I don't think I will work any more. There (sic) one pound from me and ten shillings from my sister'.

His contribution was four times his weekly benefit. He had given everything away. The Columban Fathers, who had no idea that the writer would one day be a Servant of God, were so impressed by the letter that they placed it in a special file. Today the letter is in the Vatican Library.

The Folly of Christ

Perseverance was *the* test of the Irish monks and Matt Talbot 'the old reliable' certainly passed it. 'It is constancy that God wants', he told a friend, who explained that if the weather was bad, he would go to a late Mass rather than to the first one. He lived his life of asceticism for almost forty years, largely unnoticed by his work-mates and neighbours. On reflection, he struck them as the perfect example of self-abasement - poor, clean and shabbily dressed, but always alert to the needs of others.

Towards the end of his life he seemed to live in the presence of God. 'If you spoke to Matt Talbot in the street', a neighbour remarked, 'you got the impression that you interrupted his conversation with God'. But, would this workman, who had so many monastic qualities, have qualified for the standard of 'green martyrdom'? Did he attain profound humility by adding fasting and labour to complete poverty of spirit?

Karl Rahner, the Jesuit theologian, deals with the three degrees of humility in his book, *Spiritual Exercises*, which is a commentary on St Ignatius' spiritual way. When he comes to the third degree of humility, the most profound, he writes: 'All of us cannot indulge in the folly of

Christianity in the way many of the saints in the past have done ......
conduct of this kind always demands the corresponding interior growth
and disposition - the necessary external circumstances are not enough.'

Obviously we should not look down on such extreme forms of
the following of Christ as we find in the lives of certain people, for
example, in a Matt Talbot. But we should never forget that these
things can only be done discreetly - no matter how odd they may
seem' (*Spiritual Exercises*, p. 201). Perhaps that was what Matt
envisaged when he jotted down an unusual prayer: 'O Blessed
Mother, obtain from Jesus a share in his folly'.

'A Holy, Old Man'

There was an important omission in his life which appears to point
to the wise guidance of a spiritual director. There is no evidence that
he practised corporal punishment, which was prevalent in many
Irish monasteries. Despite his long years of penance, Matt lived to
be a very old man. In the 1920's most Irish men died in their early
fifties. Matt showed the first signs of a serious illness when he was
sixty-seven. Doctors at the Mater Hospital detected what became a
serious heart condition and he was detained for a month. Later that
year, in September, 1923, he suffered a relapse and was re-admitted
and anointed. He concealed his life of asceticism and settled into the
routine of patients, receiving Holy Communion just once a week
and eating the ordinary hospital meals.

Sister Mary Dolores, who looked after him during that time, was
amazed when she discovered, years later, that she had nursed the
Servant of God. 'Matt Talbot never showed by his conduct', she said
later at the sworn inquiry of the Ordinary Process, 'that he was anything more than a sweet-natured, holy, old man'. Professor Henry
Moore, the eminent heart specialist, was Matt's doctor. He had an
opportunity to delve deeper into his patient's personality because
after his discharge from hospital in October, 1923, Matt returned as
an out-patient for regular checks. 'It occurred to me at first that he
might be a religious crank. I was not long in changing my opinion of
him. He was one of the gentlest men I have ever come across and
were it not that I was so busy at the time I should like to have had
him as a friend'. Under the influence of God's grace, 'Barney'

Talbot; the 'hard' man of O'Meara's pub, had come a long way.

This illness virtually ended Matt's working life. After his second discharge from hospital, he lived in dire poverty for eighteen months. His greatest fear was that he would be unable to pay the rent for his room and be obliged to live in an institution for paupers. Privacy was essential for his penances and devotions. Thanks to negotiations by his fellow workers in T & C Martin's, who were distressed by his condition, the firm re-employed him in the Spring of 1925. He was able only for light work and other workmen helped him when his workload became too heavy, but he had the security of a weekly wage, Within a few months Matt Talbot was dead. He died suddenly on the way to Mass on Sunday, 7th June. The cause of death was a heart attack, as doctors expected. He was sixty-nine years of age.

Totus Tuus

Matt Talbot collapsed in Granby Lane and his remains were brought to Jervis Street Hospital. While undressing the body two mortuary attendants discovered one of his secret - and most misunderstood - devotions. They found three chains, one around the waist, another around his arm and a third around his leg. It was a devotion known as the 'slavery of Jesus in Mary', which was popular in parts of Europe but not so common in Ireland. It originated in a book, *True Devotion to the Blessed Virgin*, by St Louis Marie de Montfort, a French missionary who died in 1716. Matt Talbot got a loan of this book about 1912 and he later told a friend that he discovered a devotion 'which lifted him from earth to heaven', the wearing of a chain. In the sections 236 to 242 of the book St Louis Marie points out the difference between a child of Mary and a slave of Mary: a child has rights, a slave has surrendered all. It is summarised in the motto of Pope John Paul II, *Totus Tuus,* 'Totally Yours'. A Christian who considers himself a 'slave of Mary' will live very close to his mistress and therefore very close to her Son.

St Louis Marie went on to recommend that a person practising this devotion should wear a 'little chain' as a symbol of his or her total dedication. It would act as an external reminder of the chain of sin that was broken at their baptism, and a proof that one was not ashamed of being a slave of Jesus and Mary and a sign that one had chosen the chains of love rather than the chains of sin. St Louis Marie was thinking about a bracelet, or, what is more popular today, a chain around the neck holding a medal. He even suggested that the 'little chain' might be worn either round the neck or on the arms, or around the waist or the ankle. It was primarily devotional, 'a folly of love' for Jesus and His Mother, and was not intended to be penitential.

No Half-Measure

This became Matt's special devotion. Only a few close friends knew about it. He hid the chains at home and wore them occasionally with the permission of his spiritual director from 1912. Matt was well described by a work-mate as 'a man who could not go easy at anything'. Little chains became larger chains and he wore three rather than one. It was an act of Providence that he wore them the day he died in the street.

The shock discovery began an intensive inquiry that revealed Matt Talbot's hidden life of sanctity. Had he died of a heart attack in his bed, it is probable that he would have remained unknown. Sister Dolores, who nursed him, has stated that there were no signs on Matt's body in 1923 that he wore a chain. Subsequently, Professor Moore saw no indication when he examined him during his regular checks. So the report that the chains were rusted and imbedded in his flesh is unfounded. Mary Purcell summarises the events in the mortuary in her book, *Matt Talbot and His Times*:

'The porters said that the chains were not imbedded in the flesh but that they had worn grooves on the skin'.

The Irish Dimension

There is world-wide admiration for the person who accepts an apparently superhuman challenge and succeeds. The St Brendan voyage has been hailed as one of the great maritime achievements of this century. Tim Severin and his crew emulated the reputed voyage of St Brendan and his monks to the New World, using an exact model of their little leather boat and their primitive navigational aids. That journey, fraught with many dangers, demanded exceptional initiative, courage and endurance. Some sailors thought that they were quite 'mad' to attempt it; but they were sane, dedicated men.

What they achieved in the physical order Matt Talbot achieved in the spiritual. In many ways his was a lone voyage, guided by his spiritual director. It demanded incredible faith, perseverance, humility and self-discipline. He charted his course to God, as the Irish monks did. His 'madness' is that of the saints who take the Gospel message literally and disturb the rest of us who settle for less. The clues to the mysterious aspects of his life are found in a sense of Irish history - the Irish monks' uncompromising acceptance of the need for penance and reparation, rooted in a love of God, as preached by St Patrick.

'If any man would come after me, let him deny himself and take up his cross and follow me. For whoever would save his life will lose it and whoever loses his life for my sake and the Gospel's will save it' *(Mark 8:34-35)*. All the signposts on Matt Talbot's road to God are in Irish.

For further information contact:

Hon. Secretary,
Dublin Diocesan Matt Talbot Committee,
25 Killarney Street,
Dublin 1.

Internet Web Site:- www.matt-talbot.com

BIBLIOGRAPHY

Matt Talbot and His Times
Mary Purcell (C. Goodliffe Neale)

Matt Talbot
Sir Joseph Glynn (Veritas Publications)

Irish Monasticism
Rev. John Ryan, S.J. (Talbot Press)

Old Ireland
Ed. Robert McNally, S.J. (Gill & Son)

Irish Catholics
John J. O'Riordan, C.SS.R. (Veritas Publications)

Ireland: Isle of Saints
C & B Cerbeland (Clonmore & Reynolds)

Ireland: Its Saints and Scholars
J.M. Flood (Kennikat Press)

The History of Irish Catholicism
Vol. 1 Ed. Patrick Corish (Gill & Macmillan)

The History of Ireland to The Coming of Henry II
Arthur Ua Clerigh (Kennikat Press, Port Washington)

The Modern Traveller to The Early Irish Church
Kathleen Hughes & Ann Hamlin (London SPCK)

The Course of Irish History
Ed. T.W. Moody and F.X. Martin, O.S.A. (Mercier Press)

Clonmacnois
Rev. John Ryan, S.J. (The Stationery Office)

Divided City
Curriculum Development Unit, Dublin (O'Brien Press)

True Devotion to The Blessed Virgin Mary
St Louis Marie de Montfort, (Montfort Press, Liverpool)

Spiritual Exercises
Karl Rahner, S.J. (Sheed & Ward)

Victorian Dublin
Ed. Thomas Kennedy (Albertine Kennedy Publishing)

Irish Spirituality
Ed. Michael Maher (Veritas Publications, 1981)